FREDERICK MULLER
London Melbourne Auckland Johannesburg

First published in Great Britain in 1988 by
Frederick Muller, an imprint of Century Hutchinson Ltd,
Brookmount House, 62-65 Chandos Place,
London WC2 4NW

Century Hutchinson Australia Pty Ltd
89-91 Albion Street, Surrey Hills, NSW 2070, Australia

Century Hutchinson New Zealand Limited
PO Box 40-086, Glenfield, Auckland 10, New Zealand

Century Hutchinson South Africa Pty Ltd
PO Box 337, Bergvlei, 2021 South Africa

British Library Cataloguing in Publication Data
Feigel, Marcel
    Giving up smoking is easy: I do it every day.
    1. English humorous cartoons. Collections
    from individual artists
    I. Title   II. Heaton, Brian, *1929*–
741.5′942

    ISBN 0 09 173690 0

Printed in Great Britain by
Anchor Brendon Ltd, Tiptree, Essex

Book design by Mike Coles – Studio C
Typesetting by Topic Typesetting Ltd.
Diseases by E. C. Dobson

Dedicated to Lord Ham of Morwenstow

CONTENTS

ONCE UPON A TIME

Once upon a time smoking was a very fashionable thing to do.

It had about it a sense of daring, mystery, sophistication.

Just think of Bogey getting the upper hand over Bacall while rolling a cigarette with the other.

Sinatra huddled under a lampost in the wee small hours.

Dietrich looking sultry in a smokey Blue Angel.

Or Charles Boyer soulfully gazing out of the cafe with smoke rings floating through the air.

None of these images is complete without a cigarette.

Whether it came out of a silver case or a crumpled pack, a cigarette lent a special quality to any scene.

Somehow, it intensified what was going on.

Anybody who was interesting, or <u>wanted</u> to be interesting, smoked.

5

THE ROMANCE OF SMOKE SIGNALS

More has been said with two eyes and a
cigarette than ever was said with words.
More passion expressed, more hopes
furtively relayed, even if only from a corner
of an eye in a corner of a room shrouded in a
mist of smoke.
And how many romances over the years
have begun with just three little words.
"Got a light?"

"We would smoke tipped Parliament and I loved the way he would light two together and then hand one to me."
Patricia Neal on Gary Cooper

"A cigarette is the perfect type of a perfect pleasure. It is exquisite, and it leaves one unsatisfied. What more can one want."

Oscar Wilde

THINGS ARE A LITTLE DIFFERENT NOW

Alas, times have changed.

These days a smoker's social standing ranks somewhere between a leper and a child molester.

And all too often where there's smoke there's ire.

People who you've never seen before suddenly confront you in public places.

Office mates won't sit near you.

Nice old ladies hit you with their umbrellas.

And dogs growl as you approach.

Can anyone blame you for feeling the whole world is being declared a smokeless zone?

If you want to smoke get nicked

by Peter Wilson

SMOKING has been banned at London's newest police station—unless you happen to be a prisoner or a member of the public.

The move, led by the station's senior officer, former smoker Chief Supt George Pigott, has caused ill-concealed anger among the recalcitrant smokers at Uxbridge station.

Police who want a cigarette have to slip out of their offices and go to one of four designated areas—the locker room, a lounge, a section of corridor or a first-floor room.

Even senior detectives who have their own offices are not exempt from the ban and nor are offices staffed wholly by smokers.

One officer said: "They say that reformed smokers are the worst and it's true. Since Mr Pigott gave up, he has been unable to stand the smell of smoke."

The ban began immediately the £3.400,000 station opened earlier this year and will run for at least six months before being reviewed.

Ironically, one of the few exceptions to the rigidly-enforced rule is prisoners and officers questioning them, who are allowed to smoke during interviews.

The 20-a-day officer, who refused to be named for fear of disciplinary action, said: "The rule was passed by the senior management without asking us what we thought first.

"As things stand, if you want a fag you have to go down to one of the rooms. It means the phones don't get answered and you can't carry on with your work if you want a cigarette."

From The London Evening Standard

18

TYPES OF SMOKERS

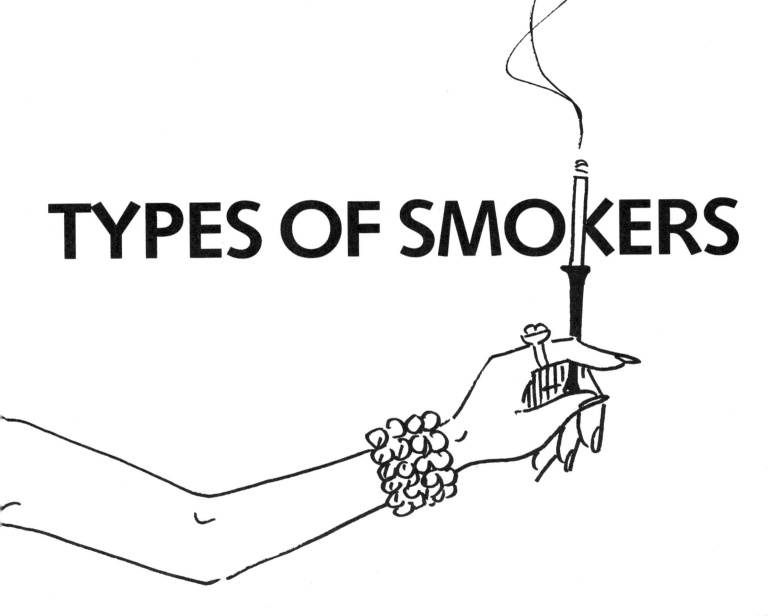

GITANE

MARLBORO

CAPSTAN FULL STRENGTH

VICEROY

DUNHILL

VIRGINIA SLIMS

SILK CUT

WINSTON

PALL MALL

SALEM

OTHER PEOPLE'S

21

23

WHO TOOK THE ASHTRAY?
(Smoking On The Sly)

As more and more places are declared off limits – including the homes of some of their best friends – smokers are faced with a serious dilemma.

What to do next.

They can either stop or resort to subterfuge. Since stopping is what we'll do tomorrow, it meals we're going to have to be particularly resourceful today.

So here are some tips on how to smoke in public without being noticed.

NOVEL WAYS OF DISGUISING CIGARETTES

Smoking in a smokeless world requires more than ingenuity. Deviousness also comes in handy.

Because what you're doing is mounting a guerilla campaign.

And in guerilla warfare camouflage is absolutely essential.

It's also important to be well armed.

And with these accessories, you'll be armed to the teeth.

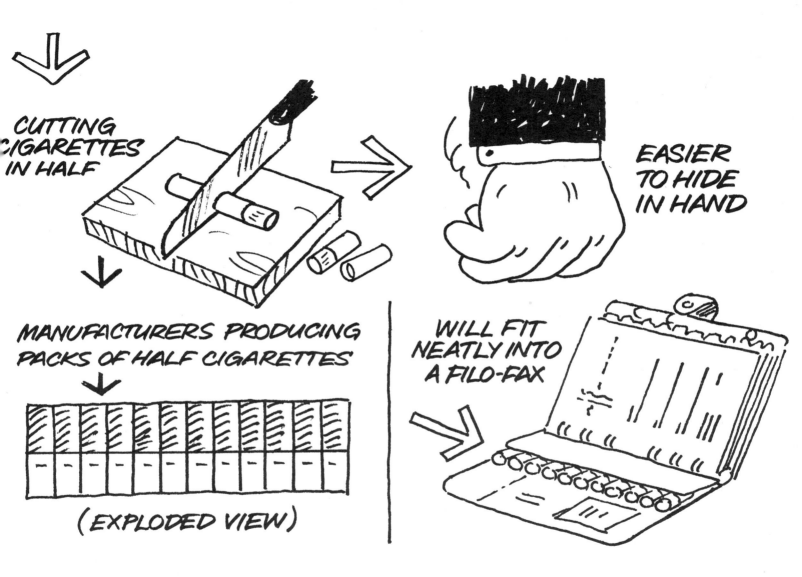

CUTTING CIGARETTES IN HALF

EASIER TO HIDE IN HAND

MANUFACTURERS PRODUCING PACKS OF HALF CIGARETTES

(EXPLODED VIEW)

WILL FIT NEATLY INTO A FILO-FAX

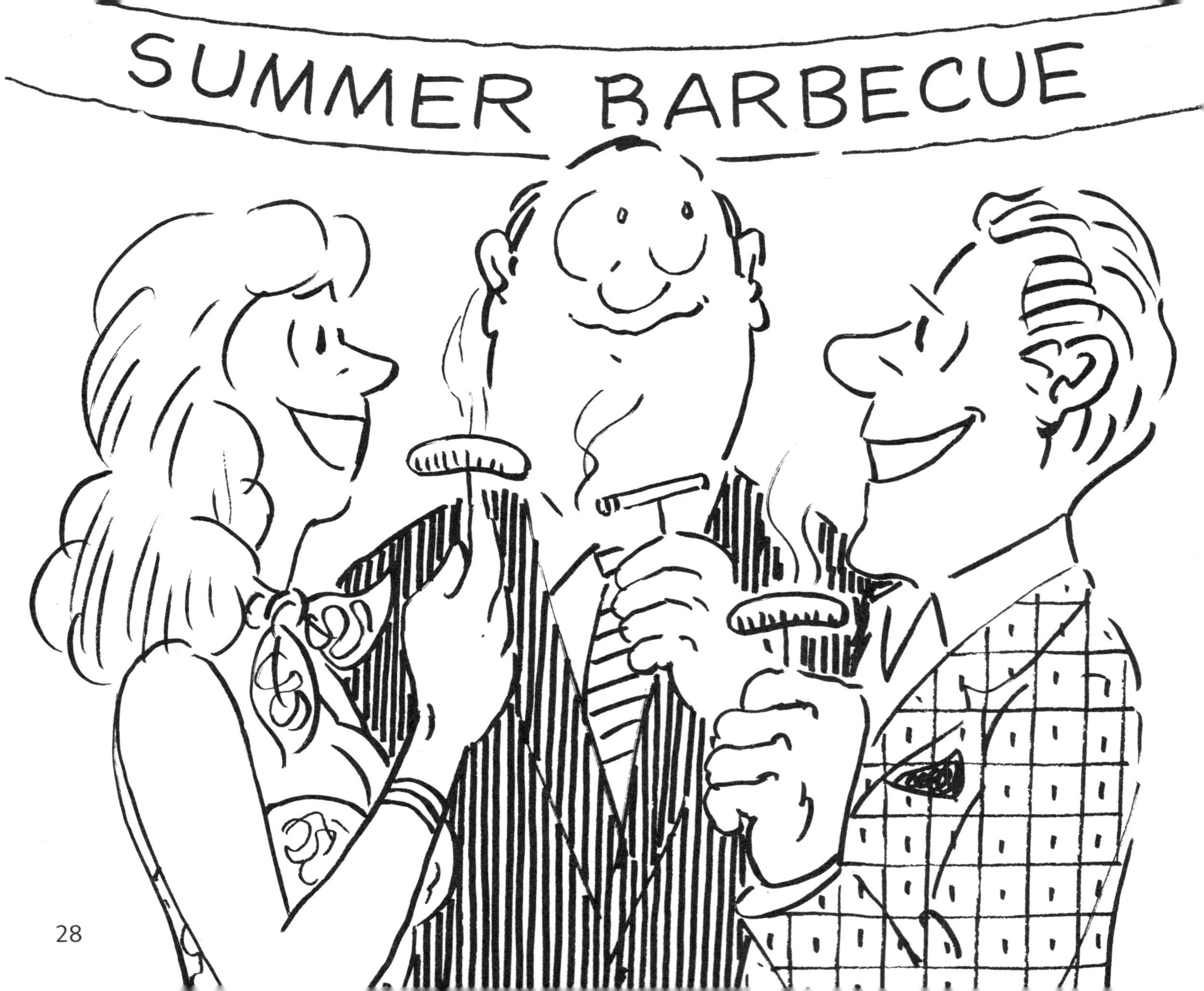
SUMMER BARBECUE

SNEAKING OFF FOR A SMOKE

One of the pleasures of tobacco is the solitary smoke. When you can quietly engage in a little reflection.
You'd think that would be a fairly simple matter to arrange.
But nowadays even having a smoke on your own is fraught with problems.
And quite frequently you find that you have to sneak off somewhere where you won't be too conspicuous.
The question is where?

THE ARMOUR
OF
HENRY VIII

PERSEPHONE

39

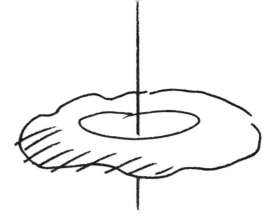

HOW TO TELL IF YOU'RE A SERIOUS SMOKER

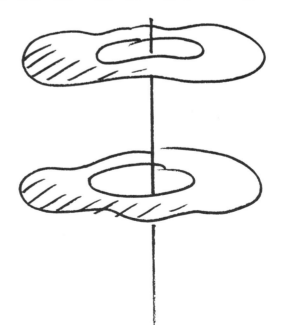

YOU START EARLY

YOU NEVER GO ANYWHERE WITHOUT TWO PACKS OF CIGARETTES

YOU LIGHT UP AS SOON AS SOMEONE ELSE DOES

That convulsive cough only smokers get, that lasts as long as a drum solo and leaves you looking like you've just been released from the Gulag after twenty years.

And when it's finally over, what do you do?

THE GRIM FACTS

One of the too frequently forgotten benefits of smoking is that it has spawned an entire industry employing thousands of people whose sole job is to analyse just how bad smoking is for you.

Since there is such a wealth of data available which is continually being updated, it must form an indispensable part of any book on smoking.

So if you're one of those people who still spits out the word 'tar' with pride and enjoy that Lee Marvin/Marianne Faithful huskiness that tobacco bestows on your voice, here are the grim facts.

DID YOU KNOW?

If you smoke,
You have <u>twice</u> as much chance of getting lung cancer.
<u>Three</u> times as much chance of getting a heart attack.
<u>Four</u> times as much chance of getting a Peptic Ulcer.
<u>Five</u> times as much chance of getting run over.
<u>Six</u> times as much chance of getting Scurvy (especially if you don't eat oranges).
<u>Seven</u> times as much chance of getting mugged.
<u>Eight</u> times as much chance of being caught by the Internal Revenue.
<u>Nine</u> times as much chance of having your aerosol cans explode on your next plane ride.
And <u>ten</u> times as much chance of finding a leak in your condom.

X-RAYS OF SMOKERS

GAULOISE

MARLBORO

DUNHILL

SILK CUT

NON SMOKER

HOW MANY PUFFS DO YOU TAKE?
(based on 20 cigarettes a day)

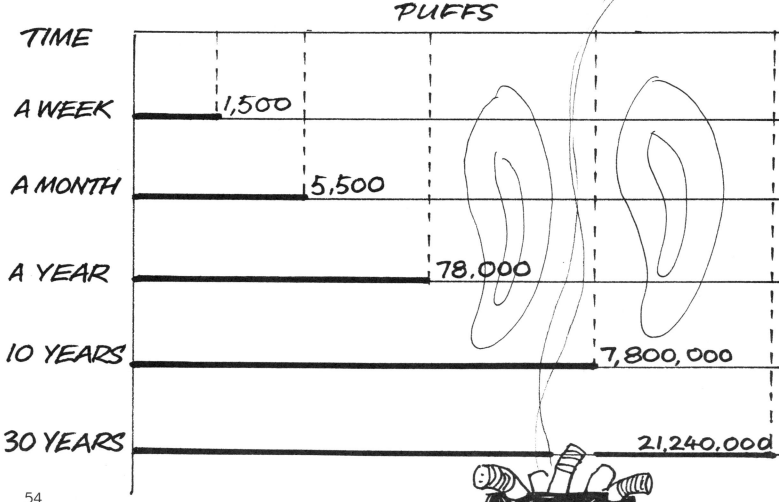

PUFFS

TIME

A WEEK	1,500
A MONTH	5,500
A YEAR	78,000
10 YEARS	7,800,000
30 YEARS	21,240,000

WHICH IS MORE DANGEROUS?

Cigarettes are worse for you than sausages but only because you consume more of them. If you were to have twenty or forty sausages a day then they would also constitute a serious health hazard, not to mention your appearance taking on a more Bavarian aspect. But most harmful of all are smoked sausages taken in quantity, particularly if you inhale.

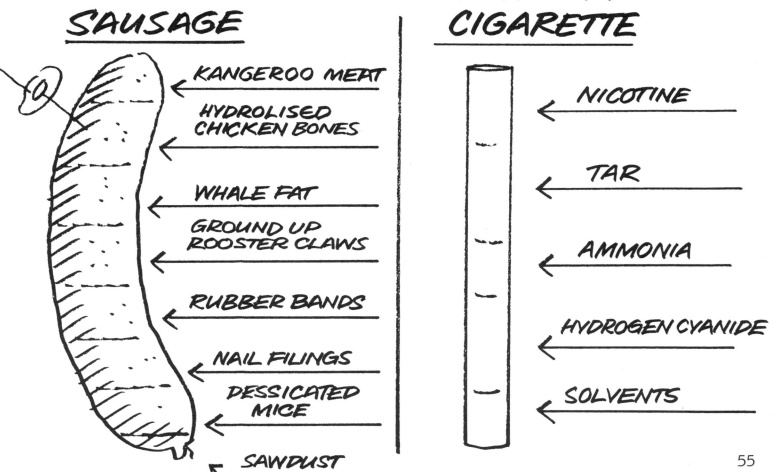

SAUSAGE

- KANGEROO MEAT
- HYDROLISED CHICKEN BONES
- WHALE FAT
- GROUND UP ROOSTER CLAWS
- RUBBER BANDS
- NAIL FILINGS
- DESSICATED MICE
- SAWDUST

CIGARETTE

- NICOTINE
- TAR
- AMMONIA
- HYDROGEN CYANIDE
- SOLVENTS

UNUSUAL DISEASES YOU CAN GET FROM SMOKING

- ACHALASIA OF THE ESOPHAGUS
- BLACKWATER FEVER
- COCK'S PECULIAR TUMOUR
- FRÖLICHS SYNDROME
- ISCHAEMIA
- PNEUMOCONIOSIS
- HAND-SCHÜLLER CHRISTIAN DISEASE
- MILROY'S DISEASE (NOT TO BE CONFUSED WITH MILDREDS)
- WILSON'S DISEASE
- ZENKER'S DEGENERATION

SPEED OF CHEMICAL REACTION

HOW QUICKLY DO YOU GET THE BUZZ?

	SECONDS										
	20	40	60	80	100	110	140	160	180	200	→
CIGARETTES	▓										
MARIJUANA	▓	▓	▓	▓	▓	▓	▓				
HEROIN	▓	▓	▓	▓	▓	▓					
ALCOHOL	▓	▓	▓	▓	▓	▓	▓	▓			
COUGH MIXTURE	▓	▓	▓	▓	▓	▓	▓	▓	▓		
COFFEE	▓	▓	▓	▓	▓	▓	▓	▓	▓		
GLUE	▓	▓	▓	▓	▓	▓	▓				
BAKED BANANAS	▓	▓	▓	▓	▓	▓	▓	▓	▓	▓	▓→
OYSTERS	▓	▓	▓	▓	▓	▓	▓	▓			
EMMENTAL ON RYE	▓										
PEPPERONI	▓	▓	▓	▓	▓	▓	▓	▓			
CHANEL Nº5	▓	▓	▓	▓	▓						

WHEN IT'S TIME TO STOP

CAN'T WALK THREE FEET WITHOUT WHEEZING

DROOPY

ASHEN FACED

SUIT LOOKS LIKE HAUNTED HOUSE

FINGERS STAINED

KICKING THE HABIT

You've finally had enough.
You've had enough of smelling like an ashtray, of being reviled by non-smokers, of being tortured by statistics, or wheezing through the night.
You've heard the arguments. You've seen the light. You're ready to trash the ash.
Now it's just a question of how.
Let's examine the various methods and see if we can find one that's right for you.

WILL POWER

This is the quickest and most decisive way to stop. And the most difficult.

One day you wake up and say "I will never smoke another cigarette."

And that's it . . . in theory.

The trouble with this method is that you need a great deal of discipline, an iron will and grim determination.

Which probably leaves you out. And most other people.

This explains why this method has such a high failure rate.

People who try this approach are the first to crack.

And once they've cracked they tend to go to pieces and often end up smoking even more than they did before.

61

WITHDRAWAL SYMPTOMS

It's three o'clock in the morning after the first day that you've given up smoking. And you're *desperate*.

You've gone through every bin and ashtray just looking for something to inhale. And you're about to try the same thing outside. Otherwise it might have to be a cab to a downtown disco just so you can buy a pack of cigarettes.

Welcome to the world of cold turkey.

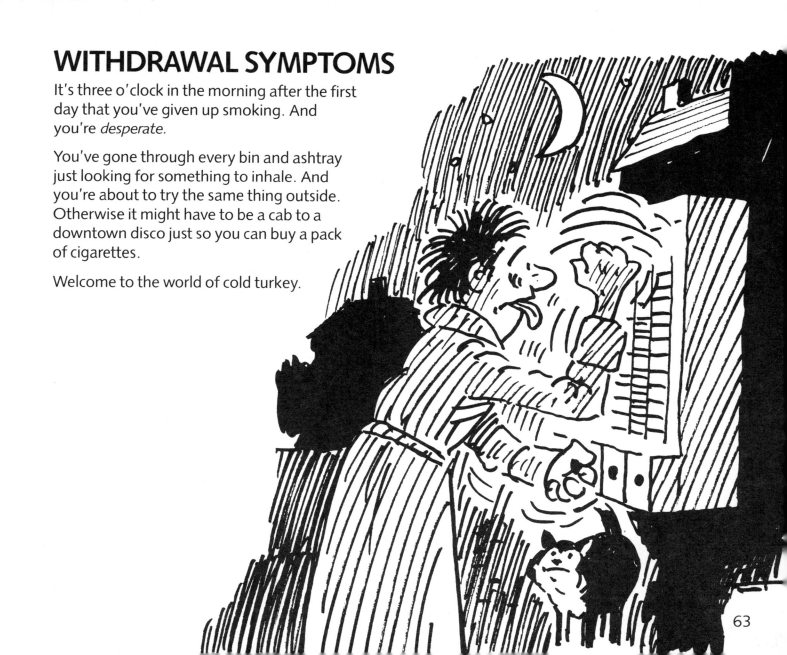

63

HERBAL CIGARETTES

They look real and they feel right and yes, you do light them. But that's as far as it goes. When the moment of truth comes, it's no contest. It's like smoking through a condom.

However, they do have their uses and can be a very effective method of getting your daily intake of vitamins particularly desiccated liver.

ACUPUNCTURE

This is an intriguing method that stops your desire for smoking by sticking needles in your body. It might have the desired effect, but it could also stop other desires. Some of which you may want to keep.

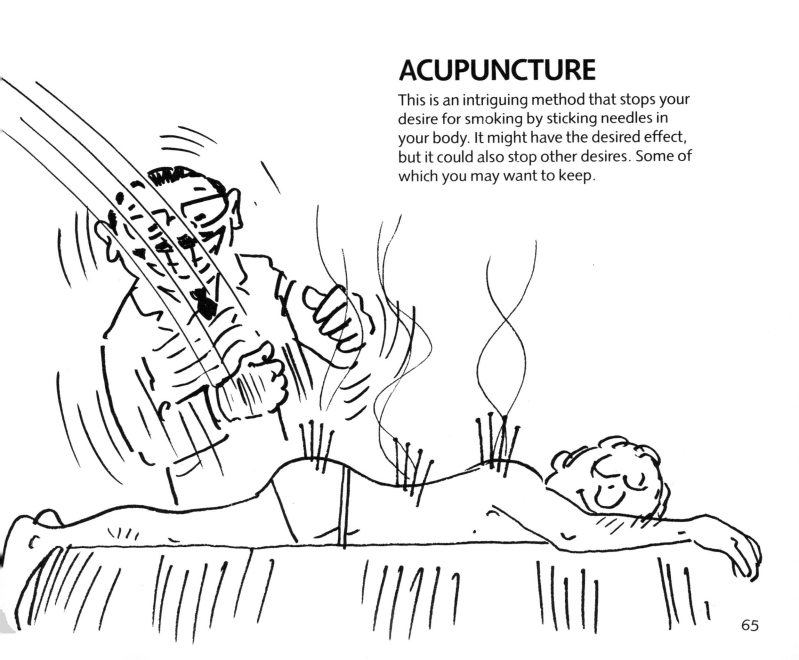

SHOCK THERAPY

WINKELSTEINS
SMOKING PREVENTION UNIT
(PATENT PENDING)

W

- EASILY ASSEMBLED.
- FROM ANY REPUTABLE D.I.Y STORE
- GUARANTEED ABSOLUTELY EFFECTIVE
- _____
- _____

N
E — W
S

CORD

CORD RELEASE

* PLEASE NOTE
CORRECT ANGLING
OF EQUIPMENT
IS ESSENTIAL

COUNTER
WEIGHT

UT · KNIFE FALLS · SECOND KNIFE · FALLS
CUTS SECOND CORD
THUNK
MALLET FALLS
REMOVE CIGARETTE, CORD RELEASED
A
CIGARETTE PACK
CONCUSSION OCCURS. THUS PREVENTING SMOKING.

SELF REVULSION

This is classic overkill otherwise known as 'aversion therapy.' With this method you smoke so much so quickly that you fill your lungs not just with nicotine but also self-loathing.

Afterwards the feeling of revulsion is so awful that you never want to touch another cigarette for as long as you live. At least until the following morning.

THE SURGICAL APPROACH

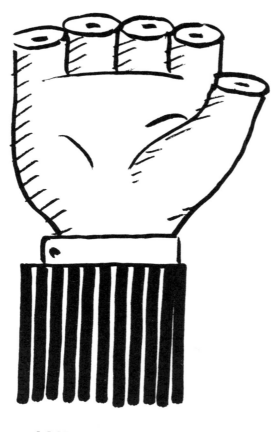

AMPUTATION

HAVING YOUR JAW WIRED

CUTTING DOWN

This is the gradual approach.
It can be very gradual. Like lighting your first
cigarette five minutes later each day, at
which rate you will have kicked the habit by
the end of the century.
Or it can mean seriously reducing your
intake to the half a dozen or so cigarettes
you really enjoy, the ones that are crucial.
That means foregoing the questionable
pleasure of the cigarette just before brushing
your teeth (or while brushing them, if you're
a really serious smoker) and others like
them.

KEY CIGARETTES OF THE DAY

You'll have to make a critical evaluation of your smoking habits (some people even suggest you write down every cigarette you smoke) and weed out the ones you smoke purely out of habit.

Having established the important cigarettes, what about the rest?

The unimportant ones you still crave. This is the hard part.

SMOKING TIME CHART

MORNING

	7. 30
	9. 00
	10. 05
	11. 35
	12

But there are little helpful tricks you can play to break the routine. Like keeping them in the attic so you have to go all the way upstairs every time you want one.
Or giving them to the children to hide.
Or, best of all, not buying any.
This not only reduces your intake but also cuts down on your friends.

TIME CONTROL CIGARETTE DISPENSER
↓

KITTY CHUNKS FOOD DISPENSER

AFTER SEX

This is a very good time to have a smoke.
After good sex it's a pleasurable way of
maintaining the glow.
After bad sex it's absolutely essential.
While after indifferent sex it's something to
get your mind off the subject.
There are some people who like to smoke
<u>during</u> sex but they tend to be either French
or Chinese.

AFTER YOU'VE STOPPED

Once you've given up, you'll notice certain changes.

Some of these are beneficial.

You'll feel fitter. You'll see what food really tastes like. And you will cough less.

You'll also go through certain bodily changes, almost as if you were going through a second adolescence (though you won't have to worry about spots).

There will also have to be certain re-adjustments in your life-style.

After all, what are going to do with your hands?

Or your mouth.

ADVANTAGES OF GIVING UP

I used to think cucumbers and bananas tasted alike.

DISADVANTAGES

I used to think my wife
was a terrific cook until I gave up smoking.

EATING

At first people who stop smoking aren't sure what to put in their mouths.

So, like a baby, they try everything – knitting needles, cocktail swizzle sticks, pens (while pretending to be deep in thought), even telephones, particularly if the call happens to be stressful.

But they soon realise that it doesn't stop the craving. So they try the next best thing.

Food.
Food is very useful. It tastes good.
You can chew it.
It keeps your hands busy and mouth happy.
So before you know it, you're eating all the time.
Snacking before dinner. Having nibbles before snacks. After Eights after dinner.
A few biscuits after nine.
You put on a stone. Then another stone.
Your hairdresser begins to comment. And all the money you're supposedly saving is going on food.
But you're not worried because you know it's only temporary.

BEFORE

AFTER

IRRITABILITY

WHAT TO DO WITH YOUR HANDS

Pretend you had a serious injury while playing rugby. You may take off the sling while sleeping or attending to matters of hygiene but make sure the bathroom door is locked.

WHAT TO DO WITH YOUR MOUTH

WHAT TO DO WITH YOUR HANDS AND MOUTH

Not recommended in public especially at board meetings, but very satisfying in a regressive sort of way especially at the end of a meal or before bed. Thumb sucking has the advantage of being both highly economical and low in calories.

REFORMED SMOKERS

In their self righteousness they are a cross between an Iranian Mullah and Margaret Thatcher. And nothing incurs their wrath like cigarette smoke which they can smell up to 200 yards.

What they should do is stay in their smoke free homes with their non-smoking friends comparing notes on the latest ionisers.

But they have more important things to do. With the tenacity of a sniffer dog and the self importance of a health inspector they make the rounds, loudly disclaiming against the evil weed, taking ashtrays wherever they go.

RELAPSE!

But life can sometimes become too much for the most zealous ex-smoker.

And one day, faced with yet another 16 hour delay on the flight to Malaga, or an overcooked steak, or someone jumping the queue at the Cashpoint machine, something snaps.

And suddenly there's a cigarette in your hand. And it's tasting good.

And before you know it, you're hooked again.

CONGRATULATIONS MRS JONES, YOUR DAUGHTER HAS JUST DELIVERED QUINS!

LINES THAT CAN YOU GET HOOKED AGAIN

A CASE HISTORY

For years Richard Lewin, knew that he was contaminating his body with all the foul, full strength tobacco that continually went through his lungs.

Then one day he decided he'd had enough and smoked his last weed.

And just like they said in the anti-smoking books, he started feeling better. For the first time in years he could taste the house wine in his local wine bar. And he could tell that the spaghetti Carbonara was made with synthetic cream instead of the real thing. And so it went. But then one day his girlfriend left him and started going out with his best friend.

Then he lost his biggest client and had to close his business. But he was strong and resisted the call of Dame Nicotine.

He tried a series of progressively more demeaning jobs until he finally went to work for the post office. But still he didn't smoke. Then his football team was relegated out of the fourth division. That was the last straw. In a moment of weakness he accepted a cigarette from a friend.

Now he's back on three packs a day. And those in-between non smoking years seem just a blur.

You would think that with all the pollution rampant in the Big Apple, a few extra fumes would hardly be noticed. But no. Hell has no fury like a New Yorker on the warpath, especially one with a cause.
And when it comes to smokers, it seems everyone's a vigilante.

HEY! WE DON'T WANT ANY REFERENCE TO SMOKING. ONCE AGAIN FROM THE TOP..
SCRIPT

107

THE FUTURE – NOT QUITE A SMOKELESS HORIZON

Although smokers are on the verge of becoming an endangered species, they will always be around.

They'll just be less noticeable.

Driven further and further back, treated like an outcast, shunted mercilessly into dark corners and dingy subterranean rooms, our smoker sits, a cigarette in his hand, staring vacantly into the distance, oblivious to the world around him.

111